WITHDRAWN

by Victor Gentle and Janet Perry

Gareth Stevens Publishing
A WORLD ALMANAC EDUCATION GROUP COMPANY

Please visit our web site at: www.garethstevens.com
For a free color catalog describing Gareth Stevens Publishing's
list of high-quality books and multimedia programs,
call 1-800-542-2595 or fax your request to (414) 332-3567.

Library of Congress Cataloging-in-Publication Data

Gentle, Victor.
    Lions / by Victor Gentle and Janet Perry.
        p. cm. — (Big cats: an imagination library series)
    Includes bibliographical references and index.
    Summary: Describes how male and female lions live, especially their hunting, mating,
and territorial behavior.
    ISBN 0-8368-3027-X (lib. bdg.)
    1. Lions—Juvenile literature. [1. Lions.] I. Perry, Janet, 1960- II. Title.
QL737.C23G483   2002
599.757—dc21   2001049695

First published in 2002 by
Gareth Stevens Publishing
A World Almanac Education Group Company
330 West Olive Street, Suite 100
Milwaukee, WI 53212 USA

Text: Victor Gentle and Janet Perry
Page layout: Victor Gentle, Janet Perry, and Tammy Gruenewald
Cover design: Tammy Gruenewald
Series editor: Catherine Gardner
Picture Researcher: Diane Laska-Swanke

Photo credits: Cover, p. 9 © Alan & Sandy Carey; pp. 5, 19 © Tom & Pat Leeson;
p. 7 © Joe McDonald/Visuals Unlimited; pp. 11, 15 © Anup Shah/BBC Natural History
Unit; p. 13 © Peter Blackwell/BBC Natural History Unit; p. 17 © Klaus-Peter Wolf/RSPCA
Photolibrary; p. 21 © Bernard Castelein/BBC Natural History Unit

Printed in the United States of America

1 2 3 4 5 6 7 8 9 06 05 04 03 02

Front cover: Two male lions gaze over the African
grasslands. Are they looking for food or females, or
are they just resting? Only they know.

TABLE OF CONTENTS

The "King of Beasts"? 4

Prides of Brides 6

Equal Work 8

Lionesses Take Their Positions 10

Get in Line 12

Lionesses and Litters, Alone 14

Males, Marks, and Mates 16

Man-Eating Lions 18

Lion-Killing Men 20

More to Read and View 22

Places to Visit, Write, or Call 22

Web Sites 23

Glossary and Index 24

Words that appear in the glossary are printed in **boldface**
type the first time they occur in the text.

THE "KING OF BEASTS"?

He has golden fur, bronze eyes that stop you in your tracks, and a long-haired mane like a crown.

The lion is one of the biggest wild cats. His thick mane circles his face and makes him look even bigger. His golden fur covers his strong body. It's not surprising that people call this cat the "king of beasts."

On grassy plains in Africa, the lion does seem to rule. He is a powerful **predator** that can kill animals as big as buffaloes and giraffes.

The lion uses his mighty roar to scare his enemies. His roar helps him find his friends, too. The lion roars louder and more often than any other wild cat.

A male lion, looking like a king. His roar can be heard as far as 4 miles (6.4 kilometers). It is as loud as the legends claim — but it's real!

PRIDES OF BRIDES

Unlike other wild cats, lions do not live alone. They live in large family groups, or **prides**. Prides have one to three male lions, two to twenty females, called **lionesses**, and all of their **cubs**.

Most of the time, all the members of the pride get along well. Together, they find food, protect their **territory**, and care for their cubs. Lions have a better chance to survive because they live in a pride.

A pride of lionesses rests with their cubs. Most cubs die before they grow up. Being in a pride helps survivors live longer.

EQUAL WORK

Some prides have lived in the same territory for 20 years. Mothers, daughters, granddaughters, and female cousins live together their whole lives. When old lionesses die, the younger ones keep the pride going.

Lionesses and lions share the work of the pride. Lionesses do not "obey" the males. Usually, the lionesses do the hunting and take care of the cubs. Male lions protect the pride's territory from predators — and from other lions.

This male rubs a tree to leave his scent on it. That warns other males who might fight him — or kill his cubs.

LIONESSES TAKE THEIR POSITIONS

Lionesses choose when and where to hunt. They follow herds of **prey**, such as zebras, as the herds move. Then, lionesses use teamwork.

Lionesses slowly surround a herd of prey. They get close enough to find weak or slow ones — or scare one or more from the herd. Then, the lionesses take their positions. The "wings" go to the edges of the herd and keep the prey moving toward the "centers," the lionesses who capture the prey. Males usually watch the hunt and wait until after the kill to eat.

A lioness chases a zebra. If the pride is lucky, two teams hunt two zebras at the same time.

GET IN LINE

Members of the pride work together to catch prey. But they do not share equally when it is time to eat. Male lions are the biggest and strongest, so they eat first. Lionesses eat next. The bossiest cubs eat after them. Hurt, sick, and small lions eat last.

Jackals and other wild dogs, **hyenas**, vultures, and leopards sometimes steal food before the cubs eat. Leopards, jackals, and wild dogs also will kill lion cubs if they get the chance. Lions may be the "king of beasts," but lion cubs have many enemies.

A male lion and cubs eat a zebra. Most often, lions eat wildebeests, gazelles, warthogs, and zebras. They kill the biggest possible prey they can.

LIONESSES AND LITTERS, ALONE

Two to four cubs are born in a **litter**. When the cubs are born, they are helpless. The lioness hides them in a **den**. She must move her cubs often. Predators that find her den will eat the cubs.

When cubs grow strong enough, they join the pride. Any lioness will **nurse** any cub in the pride. At six months old, cubs stop drinking milk. They must fight for the food the lionesses bring.

Mothers and cubs take a stroll. Lionesses in a pride have cubs all at the same time, so all the cubs in the pride are about the same age.

MALES, MARKS, AND MATES

Lion brothers and male cousins team up, too. They leave their **birth pride** when they are almost two years old. They travel in twos or threes. They hunt together and defend each other. They fight other males for the right to move into a pride and **mate** with the lionesses.

When male lions join a pride, they **mark** their territory to warn other males not to hunt there. On rare occasions, males help bring down very large prey, such as giraffes and water buffaloes. Males also protect the pride from predators who try to steal food or kill the lion cubs.

These young male lions live on their own right now. Males leave their birth prides to mate with females of other prides.

MAN-EATING LIONS

Lions look for prey that is easy for them to find and catch. Near a town, the easiest meal for a starving lion *might* be a person.

In the 1800s, two brother lions killed more than 125 railway workers on the Tsavo plains in eastern Africa. The Tsavo lions were shot because they had killed people. These fearsome man-eating lions are famous.

In fact, very few lions kill people for food. On the savannas of Africa, they hunt wildebeests, warthogs, gazelles, zebras, and other prey.

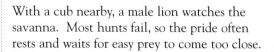

With a cub nearby, a male lion watches the savanna. Most hunts fail, so the pride often rests and waits for easy prey to come too close.

LION-KILLING MEN

Many people kill lions — for fun, not food. Lions were almost wiped out by 1900 — just so hunters could put lion heads on their walls and lion skins on their floors. Once, wild lions lived in Europe, Africa, India, China, and Arabia. Now, they live in the wild only in Africa and India. Hunters wiped out all wild Barbary lions.

Lions never kill to decorate their homes. They never wiped out any group of prey. And yet, lions are in danger of **extinction**. Lions living in the wild are a treasure the world will lose if people are not careful.

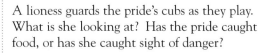

A lioness guards the pride's cubs as they play. What is she looking at? Has the pride caught food, or has she caught sight of danger?

MORE TO READ AND VIEW

Books (Nonfiction) *Big Cats* (series). Victor Gentle and Janet Perry (Gareth Stevens)
Elsa. Joy Adamson (Pantheon)
How to Hide a Polar Bear and Other Mammals. Ruth Heller
  (Grosset & Dunlap)
How Wild Animals Fight. Dorothy Shuttlesworth (Doubleday)
The Lion Family Book. Angelika Hofer & Gunter Ziesler
  (Picture Book Studio)
The Lion and the Savannah. J. David Taylor (Crabtree)

Books (Activity) *Drawing the Big Cats.* Paul Frame (Franklin Watts)

Books (Fiction) *Jambi and the Lions.* Jennifer Brady (Landmark Editions)
Nanta's Lion. Suse MacDonald (Morrow Junior Books)

Videos (Nonfiction) *Animals of Africa.* (Celebrity Home Entertainment)
Swinging Safari. (National Geographic)
Tao the Lion. (National Geographic Television)

PLACES TO VISIT, WRITE, OR CALL

Lions live at the following zoos. Call or write to the zoos to find out about their lions and their plans to preserve lions in the wild. Better yet, go see the lions, person to cat!

St. Louis Zoo
1 Government Drive
St. Louis, MO 63110-1395
(314) 781-0900

Papanack Park Zoo
150 Nine Mile Road
Wendover, ON
Canada KOA 3KO
(613) 673-7275

Woodland Park Zoo
5500 Phinney Avenue North
Seattle, WA 98103-5897
(206) 684-4880

Memphis Zoo
2000 Prentiss Place
Memphis, TN 38112
(901) 276-WILD

WEB SITES

Web sites change frequently, but we believe the following web sites are going to last. You also can use a good search engine, such as **Yahooligans!** [*www.yahooligans.com*] or **Google** [*www.google.com*], to find more information about lions, other big cats around the world, and their homes. Some keywords that will help you are: *lions, savannas, cats, African wildlife, zoo animals,* and *endangered species.*

www.yahooligans.com
Yahooligans! is a great research tool. It has a lot of information and plenty to do. Under <u>Science and Nature</u>, click on <u>Animals</u> and then click on <u>The Big Picture: Animals</u>. From there, you can try <u>Animal Videos</u>, <u>Endangered Animals</u>, <u>Animal Bytes</u>, <u>BBC Animals</u>, or <u>Natural History Notebooks</u> and search for information about lions, savannas, and African wildlife.

www.asiatic-lion.org/gallery1.html
The *Asiatic Lion Information Center* gallery has pictures of the Asiatic Lion.

www.aristotle.net/~swarmack/nslions.html
On the *Not So Grateful Dead* site, you can see a *living* Barbary lion. He was kept as a "pet" by an emporer. Now, this lion and a few others live in a zoo. It is not known whether other Barbary lions exist.

library.thinkquest.org/12353
ThinkQuest will show you what other kids are finding out and writing about lions. Just click on <u>African Mammals</u>.

www.super-kids.com
Super-Kids will take you to games and pictures of big cats, along with other information about big cats. Start by clicking on <u>Animals</u>. Then, try <u>Africa</u>, <u>Monkeys</u>, <u>Tigers</u>, or <u>Zoos</u>.

www.leopardsetc.com/meet.html
Leopards, Etc. lets you hear big cats. Click on the speaker icon next to each cat name. You can hear all kinds of big cats roaring, growling, rasping, barking, and purring.

www.nationalgeographic.com/features/97/cats/
National Geographic has a really cool game that lets you design the perfect predator.

www.nhm.org/cats/
The Natural History Museum of Los Angeles County has a really great exhibit called *Cats! Mild to Wild.* Click on <u>Biology</u>, and you will find how cats are built, how they use their claws, teeth, legs, and voices — and more!

GLOSSARY

You can find these words on the pages listed. Reading a word in a sentence helps you understand it even better.

birth pride (BURTH PRYED) — the family group of lions into which a cub is born and grows up 16

cubs (KUHBZ) — big cats' babies 6, 8, 12, 14, 16, 18, 20

den (DEN) — the place where animals give birth, hide their cubs, and sleep 14

extinction (ex-TINKT-shun) — the end of life for a whole type of animal 20

hyenas (hye-EE-nuhs) — predators with powerful jaws and short hind legs 12

lionesses (LYE-uh-ness-es) — female lions 6, 8, 10, 12, 14, 16, 20

litter (LIT-ur) — a group of cubs born at the same time to the same mother 14

mark (MARK) — to leave a scent or scratches to warn other animals that a territory already belongs to a pride 16

mate (MAYT) — come together to make babies 16

nurse (NURS) — to feed milk to cubs 14

predator (PRED-uh-tur) — an animal that hunts other animals for food 4, 8, 14, 16

prey (PRAY) — animals that are hunted by other animals for food 10, 12, 16, 18, 20

prides (PRYEDZ) — groups of lionesses, their cubs and, from time to time, one to three males 6, 8, 12, 14, 16, 18, 20

territory (TER-uh-tor-ee) — an area of land that an animal (or animal group) marks out as its hunting ground 6, 8, 16

INDEX

Africa 4, 18, 20
age 14

Barbary lions 20

enemies 4, 12

females 6, 8, 10, 12, 14, 16
food 6, 10, 12, 14, 16, 18, 20
fur 4
gazelles 12, 18

hunters 20
hunting 8, 10, 16, 18

India 20

jackals 12

leopards 12

males 4, 6, 8, 10, 12, 16, 18
mane 4
man-eating lions 18

roar 4

Tsavo plains 18

vultures 12

warthogs 12, 18
wild dogs 12
wildebeests 12, 18

zebras 10, 12, 18